God
Awaits You

Ms. Marie Kelly
26 Locust Dr. Apt. 35
Summit, NJ 07901

Titles in the *Thirty Days with a Great Spiritual Teacher* series

ALL WILL BE WELL
Based on the Classic Spirituality of *Julian of Norwich*

GOD AWAITS YOU
Based on the Classic Spirituality of *Meister Eckhart*

LET NOTHING DISTURB YOU
A Journey to the Center of the Soul with *Teresa of Avila*

PEACE OF HEART
Based on the Life and Teachings of *Francis of Assisi*

TRUE SERENITY
Based on Thomas A Kempis' *The Imitation of Christ*

YOU SHALL NOT WANT
A Spiritual Journey Based on *The Psalms*

Future titles in the series will focus on authors and classic works such as
Hildegaard of Bingen, John of the Cross, The Cloud of Unknowing, Augustine,
Catherine of Sienna, Brother Lawrence, and others.

30 Days with a Great Spiritual Teacher

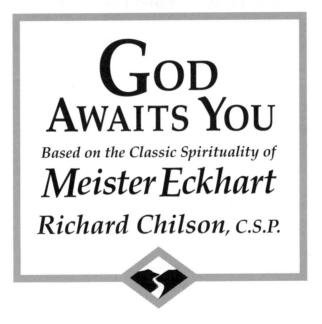

GOD AWAITS YOU

Based on the Classic Spirituality of

Meister Eckhart

Richard Chilson, C.S.P.

AVE MARIA PRESS Notre Dame, Indiana 46556

Richard Chilson is the author of over a dozen books on Catholicism and world religions. He currently serves as a chaplain at the University of California at Berkeley.

The passages from Meister Eckhart are contemporary English translations and paraphrases developed from a variety of original sources.

Copyright © 1996 Quest Associates

All rights reserved. No part of this book may be used or reproduced in any manner whatsoever, except in the case of brief excerpts in the context of reviews, without written permission of the publisher, Ave Maria Press, Inc., Notre Dame, IN 46556.

International Standard Book Number: 0-87793-572-6

Library of Congress Card Number: 95-80888

Cover and text design by Elizabeth J. French

Printed and bound in the United States of America

Contents

A sick man was once asked
why he did not ask God to heal him of his affliction.
He replied,
"First, I am sure that our loving God
would not have made me sick
if it were not best for me.
Second, it would be wrong
to wish for my will rather than
God's will for me.
Third, why should
I ask the rich, loving, and generous God
for such a small thing?"

Meister Eckhart

Meister Eckhart is finally emerging from the shadow of heresy cast over him in his own day and reinforced by Pope John XXII before his death. Today he is even quoted frequently by Pope John Paul II, a sign that his teaching is once again in favor. In addition to his acceptance among Catholics, he has also become a significant bridge between the Eastern and Western mystical traditions. Eckhart's writing is not as exclusively Christian as that of other mystics such as John of the Cross or Teresa of Avila. At times, it is hard to differentiate his thought from that of a Zen Buddhist. This is not due to any absence of Christian faith, but to the fact that he prefers a more abstract language to traditional biblical images.

Eckhart fell out of favor for a number of reasons. As is often the case with mystics, Eckhart struggled with the tension between his own direct experience of the divine and the culture of the church and time in which he lived. Most people are content to accept the truths of their religious tradition as taught by its authorities and do not seek their own experience of God. As an exception to this approach mystics have generally been suspect, at least in their day, and only approved once they are safely dead. Such was the case with Thomas Aquinas, Teresa of Avila, and John of the Cross with the Roman Catholic tradition, and John Wesley, Jacob Boehme, and George Fox within Protestantism.

But if being a mystic is dangerous, a mystic who commands a following and who lives at a time of spiritual awakening, as did Meister Eckhart, is doubly suspect. Eckhart did not write for the monastic elite. He was a member of the Dominicans, the Order of Preachers, and his audience was the ordinary people to whom he preached. The fact that Eckhart lived in a time of spiritual renewal is evidenced by the formation of numerous religious communities in his area, the Rhine valley. Among these were the Beghards, the Friends of God, and a women's community with whom he was especially popular, the Beguines.

Like his contemporary Dante, Eckhart wrote not only in Latin, the official language of the church, but in German, the language of the people. He brought mysticism to the masses and thus provoked concern among some of the hierarchy that his ideas, even if orthodox in themselves, might be misinterpreted.

Eckhart was born in the German village of Hochheim in 1260 and died about 1328. Since he does not disclose personal details in his writings, we know very little of his life. We do know that he entered the Dominican Order during his teens, that he studied for the priesthood, and was familiar with the work of another Dominican, Thomas Aquinas, who had just died.

At that time Aquinas himself was under a cloud of suspicion. While Aquinas has since become the most highly regarded of all Catholic theologians, Eckhart's rehabilitation has taken significantly longer. But both men were essentially mystics. While Aquinas is remembered most for his theological ability, we should also keep in mind that he refused to complete his greatest work, the Summa Theologica, because of a mystical experience in which he came to see all his wonderful words as only straw in comparison with the gold of the divine vision.

When Eckhart was about thirty-five years old he was

appointed prior of Erfurt. About this time he wrote *Talks on Spiritual Instruction*, the first book from which our selections are taken: We are told in the preface that they are conferences which "the prior of Erfurt, Brother Eckhart, gave to those of his students who had asked about spiritual matters when they sat around the table in the evening."

In others words, these are basic counsels concerning the spiritual life and the path which a person follows in drawing closer to God. Here Eckhart is practical and down-to-earth. Many of the things he discusses resonate with questions we have today about beginning a spiritual life. Again and again in these talks the master warns us not to forget the essentials. It is all too easy to mistake the trees for the forest, to get bogged down in techniques and ideas and miss the essence of all spiritual life, our relationship to God.

The Dominicans came to recognize Eckhart's genius and sent him to the great University of Paris where he received his Licentiate and Master's degree. This is the origin of his title "Meister," ever after attached to his name. He soon became provincial of the Dominicans in Saxony where other responsibilities also fell upon him.

During this period he wrote *The Book of Blessings and Comforts,* the source of the other selections in this volume. Tradition says that it was written for the Queen of Hungary who had suffered a series of tragic mishaps. The book focuses upon suffering and evil and aims not so much to comfort as to offer a clear presentation of how a person who is engaged in spiritual work might deal with adversity.

Both *Talks on Spiritual Instruction* and *The Book of Blessings and Comfort,* are very practical. They focus upon the nature of the spiritual life. Eckhart, though a true mystic, does not provide poetry and vision for his students. Rather he offers hard, practical advice on how to discern one's spiritual path, how to follow that path, how to do the work required. He douses the reader with a refreshing splash of cold water: if you want intimacy with God, here is what you have to do. Given much of the feel-good, wishy-washy pabulum that currently passes for spiritual guidance, Eckhart is a wonderful alternative.

His appeal to modern readers and the suspicion he labored under during his lifetime may be due to the same cause—he cuts immediately to the quick. For Eckhart, God and God alone is reality. Anything else is at best a means or at worst an obstacle. In this way he is very like the masters of Zen Buddhism. With time, any religion, any culture, any individual picks up baggage. After a while it is easy to overestimate the baggage's importance. Eckhart will not let us do this. He constantly holds before us the only matter of substance, the only reality: our relationship to God.

How to Pray This Book

The purpose of this book is to open a gate for you, to make accessible the spiritual experience and wisdom of one of history's most important spiritual teachers, Meister Eckhart.

This is not a book for mere reading. It invites you to meditate and pray its words on a daily basis over a period of thirty days.

It is a handbook for a spiritual journey.

Before you read the "suggestions" for taking this spiritual journey, remember that this book is meant to free your spirit, not confine it. If on any day the meditation does not resonate well for you, turn elsewhere to find a passage which seems to best fit the spirit of your day and your soul. Don't hesitate to repeat a day as often as you like until you feel that you have discovered what the Spirit, through the words of the author, has to say to your spirit.

Here are suggestions on one way to use this book as a cornerstone of your prayers.

As Your Day Begins

As the day begins set aside a quiet moment in a quiet place to read the meditation suggested for the day.

The passage is short. It never runs more than a couple of hundred words, but it has been carefully selected to give a spiritual focus, a spiritual center to your whole day. It is designed to remind you as another day begins of your own existence at a spiritual level. It is meant to put you in the presence of the spiritual master who is your companion and teacher on this journey. But most of all the purpose of the passage is to remind you that at this moment and at every moment during this day you will be living and acting in the presence of a God who invites you continually, but quietly, to live in and through him.

A word of advice: read slowly. Very slowly. The meditation has been broken down into sense lines to help you do just this. Don't read to get to the end, but to savor each part of the meditation. You never know what short phrase, what word will trigger a response in your spirit. Give the words a chance. After all, you are not just reading this passage, you are praying it. You are establishing a mood of serenity for your whole day. What's the rush?

All Through Your Day

Immediately following the day's reading you will find a single sentence which we call a mantra, a word borrowed from the Hindu tradition. This phrase is meant as a companion for your spirit as it moves through a busy day. Write it down on a 3" x 5" card or on the appropriate page of your daybook. Look at it as often as you can. Repeat it quietly to yourself and go on your way.

It is not meant to stop you in your tracks or to distract you from responsibilities, but simply, gently to remind you of the presence of God and your desire to respond to this presence.

As Your Day Is Ending

This is a time for letting go of the day. Find a quiet place and quiet your spirit. Breathe deeply. Inhale, exhale—slowly and deliberately, again and again until you feel your body let go of its tension.

Read the questions which are presented for you as a way of

reviewing your day in the light of the meditation. Answer them slowly, thoughtfully, without anxiety or stress. They are not a test, but simply a way of concentrating the spiritual energy of your day as it comes to an end.

When you are ready, read the evening prayer slowly, phrase by phrase. You will find in it phrases to remind you of the meditation with which you began the day and the mantra that has accompanied you all through your day.

It is a time for summary and closure. Invite God to embrace you with love and to protect you through the night. Sleep well.

Some Other Ways to Use This Book

1. Use it any way your spirit suggests. As mentioned earlier, skip a
    passage that doesn't resonate for you on a given day, or repeat
    for a second day or even several days a passage whose richness
    speaks to you. The truths of a spiritual life are not absorbed in a
    day, or for that matter, in a lifetime. So take your time. Be patient
    with the Lord. Be patient with yourself.

2. Take two passages and/or their mantras—the more contrasting
    the better—and "bang" them together. Spend time discovering
    how their similarities or differences illumine your path.

3. Start a spiritual journal to record and deepen your experience of
    this thirty-day journey. Using either the mantra or another
    phrase from the reading that appeals to you, write a spiritual

account of your day, a spiritual reflection. Create your own meditation.

4. Join millions who are seeking to deepen their spiritual life by joining with others to form a small group. More and more people are doing just this to support each other in their mutual quest. Meet once a week, or at least every other week to discuss and pray about one of the meditations. There are many books and guides available to help you make such a group effective.

Thirty Days with
Meister Eckhart

Day One

My Day Begins

True Obedience

Real obedience is the highest of all the virtues.
No great work can be brought to fulfillment without it.
All tasks, however great or trivial,
are improved by this discipline of obedience.
To be obedient is to be carefree;
to be obedient is to be filled with bliss.
When we purify ourselves
God, by nature, flows into us;
when we surrender our own will

we invite God to will for us
what God would will for God's self.
And God is obliged to will for me,
because to do otherwise
would be to neglect me,
and in the process neglect God's self.

When I give up choosing for myself,
God can choose for me.
And what will God choose for me?
God will choose that I should not choose for myself.

When I deny myself
God's will becomes the same as my own will.
An obedient person never says,
"This is what I want."
An obedient person seeks only to deny self.

Such a person will not ask
to be made virtuous
or to be given eternal life.
This person asks to know
only what God desires.
And such a prayer is infinitely superior
to the previous ways of praying.

God's true disciple is not pleased
when someone gives her something
or tells him what he wishes to hear.

Our only desire
is what is most pleasing to God.

All Through the Day

When I give up choosing for myself,
God can choose for me.

My Day Is Ending

Take a few minutes to look back over your day.

Can you remember moments of surrender?

What were they like?

What about moments of resistance?

Night Prayer

Lord, help me to surrender
all of myself to you.
Allow my will
to always follow
your will.
Guide me along your way
and give me the strength to follow.

8/21/18

Day Two

◆◆◆◆◆

My Day Begins

The Best Prayer

The most powerful prayer
which can accomplish almost anything,
and the greatest action a person can achieve,
both arise out of a pure heart.
The purer our hearts,
the more powerful, the more illustrious,
useful, praiseworthy, and whole
are both our prayer and our action.

A pure heart knows no bounds to its capabilities.
But what constitutes a pure heart?
A pure heart is unencumbered, without worry,
and not attached to things.
It does not desire to have its own way,
but is content to be immersed in God's loving will.
A pure heart is forgetful of self.
No work is too trivial to be lifted up
in its power and importance by a pure heart.
So let our prayer be that every part of our being—
our minds, eyes, ears, mouth, heart, limbs and senses—
strive to bring us purity of heart.
And let us not cease from praying
until we find ourselves in unity with God
to whom all our prayers and attention tend.

A mind completely devoted to God is
the foundation of goodness for human nature and spirit.
Strive that God should be great in you,
be zealous for God in all your comings and goings.
Hold fast to God
and God will bring about every good thing.
If you seek God, you will find God
together with every good thing.
What you sought before, now seeks you.
What you once pursued, now pursues you.
What you once fled, now flees you.
Everything comes to the person
who really approaches God,
bringing all that is God with it,
and causing all that is alien to God to fly away.

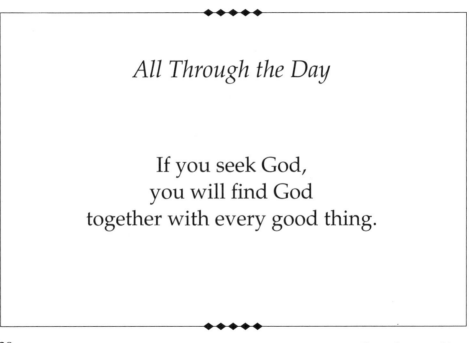

All Through the Day

If you seek God,
you will find God
together with every good thing.

My Day Is Ending

Take a moment to relax and let go now.

Recall some time or incident today
when you were anxious or worried.

Relive that incident now and imagine
yourself there without worry or anxiety.

How is this way different?

Night Prayer

God, help me to find a pure heart
with which to love you
and all creation.
Let me forget myself
in your service.

Day Three

My Day Begins

Solitude or Society

Someone once asked me:
"Some people prefer solitude;
they say their peace of mind depends upon this.
But wouldn't they be better off in church?"
My answer was no.
I shall explain why.
If you do well, you do well wherever you are,
and in whatever surroundings;

and if you fail, you fail wherever you are,
and in whatever surroundings.
If you succeed, God is truly within you,
and God is with you everywhere,
in the marketplace
as much as in church or in seclusion.

If you truly have God and only God,
nothing will disturb you. Why?
Because you are totally focused upon God
and only God.
Therefore everything is nothing but God to you.
You reveal God in every action, in every situation.
All your activities point to God.
Your works depend upon God for their authority
and not upon yourself;

for you are merely the agent.
If your intention is God and only God,
then God does what you do
and nothing can disturb you,
neither society nor surroundings.
And no person can disturb you,
for you consider nothing,
look for nothing, relish nothing other than God,
who is with you in your perfect dedication.
And since God is not distracted
by a multiplicity of things,
neither can you be,
for you are in God, in whom
all things are gathered into unity
and brought to completion.

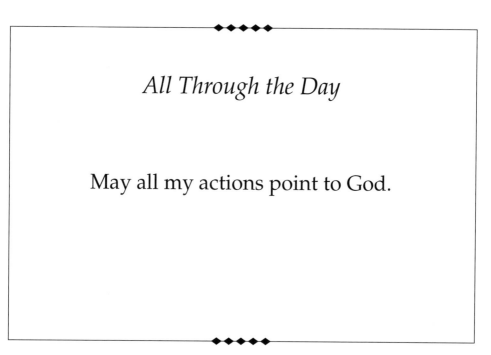

All Through the Day

May all my actions point to God.

My Day Is Ending

When did you feel closest to God today?
Relive that moment now.

When did you feel farthest from God today?
Relive that moment now.

As you do, imagine that
you are closest to God in this event.

Night Prayer

May all my actions
speak of you, Lord.
May my heart show forth
only you.
May my words proclaim
only you.

Day Four

My Day Begins
Oneness of Mind Is All

Keep hold of God in everything
and train your mind to keep God always
in your feelings, thoughts, and desires.

Take care how you think of God.
Try to think of God everywhere
in the same way you think of God
when you feel particularly close to God.

Take God with you
into the crowds and rat race of the secular world.

I do not imply that the marketplace
is more important than church,
or business more important than meditation.
But preserve the same mind,
the same trust,
the same zeal for God in all your affairs.
If you maintain this equanimity in all things,
nothing can separate you from the presence of God.
On the other hand,
if you are not conscious of God's presence,
but need to be always reading books about God
from this or that author,
or have to find God by special methods,
a special technique, person, or place;
believe me, you have not yet found God.

You will be easily sidetracked
for you do not yet seek, think, and love only God.
Therefore anything can be your stumbling block:
evil company or good,
marketplace or church,
bad deeds and words as well as good ones.
Your difficulty arises from that fact
that God is not yet everything to you.
If God were everything,
you would get along well wherever you went,
among whatever people.
You would be in God
and no one could disturb you
or stop God's working in you.

All Through the Day

If God were everything to me,
nothing could disturb me.

My Day Is Ending

Take a moment to recall
when you felt closest to God today.

Let the experience expand as you remember it.

Now imagine taking that feeling of closeness
into some other moments of the day.
How do things change?

Night Prayer

Lord, you are always close to me,
although I may not be close to you,
or feel your presence.
Let me be content with
my current spiritual state,
knowing that you are leading me
wherever you will best for me.

Day Five

◆◆◆◆◆

My Day Begins

To Truly Possess God

What is it like to truly possess God?

Such possession is grounded in the heart;
it includes an inner, intellectual return to God.
It does not depend upon
any specific method of contemplation.
It is impossible to keep such a method in mind,
or at least it is very difficult,
and even then it is not for the best.

Do not let yourself be satisfied
with the God you can conceive,
for when that thought slips your mind,
the God you conceived slips away too.
You do not want your thought of God,
but rather that reality of God as God is,
who is far above every human thought or creature.
When we open ourselves to God as God really is,
then God does not slip away
unless we turn away of our own will.

When you open yourself to God's divinity and otherness,
when you allow the reality of God to enter you,
God illuminates everything.
Everything tastes of God and shines forth God.
God continually shines in your heart.

You will come to share
the disinterest, detachment,
and spiritual vision of your heart's delight,
the ever present God.
You will thirst with a true thirst,
and drinking will be your zeal,
even when you are preoccupied with other matters.

Wherever you are,
with whomever you are,
whatever your intentions, thoughts, or activities,
drinking will be your desire
as long as the thirst endures.
The greater the thirst,
the more prominent and deep-seated
the hope of the drink will be.

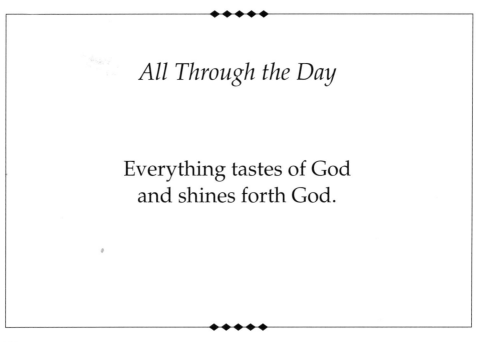

All Through the Day

Everything tastes of God
and shines forth God.

My Day Is Ending

Take a moment or two to relax.

Imagine the day receding with each out breath.

Imagine taking in God with each in breath.

How have you tasted God today?

How has God shone forth for you today?

Night Prayer

Gracious God,
your whole creation shines forth
with your splendor.
May I breathe that glory in and out
so that I am transformed by you,
and totally drowned in your splendor.

Day Six

My Day Begins

The Art of Prayer

Let us say that you love something
with your whole being,
so that nothing or no one else can give you joy.
No matter where you are or who you are with,
your beloved will not be out of mind.
You will see the beloved everywhere,
and the more your love grows,
the more vividly you will see the beloved

everywhere and in everyone.
You will never consider taking a rest
because you are never tired of your love.

So the more we see everything as of God,
the more God finds pleasure with us.
Seeing in this way demands discipline and love,
a concern for the spiritual path,
and a wakeful, honest scrutiny
of the way you perceive people and objects.
You cannot learn this discipline
by running away from the world.
But you must learn how to cultivate an inner solitude
wherever and with whomever you find yourself.
You must learn to look deeply into things
and discover God there;

you must plant a firm impression of God in your mind
and hold it there constantly.
It is like acquiring any art such as learning to write.
You must practice constantly whether you want to or not,
whether it is easy or not.
Through faithful practice you learn to write
and acquire the art of penmanship.
With time you will learn to write fluently and with style.
The accomplished scribe
does not have to be constantly conscious of her skill,
and so she creates her art by means of it.
So you should shimmer with the divine presence
without having to work at it.
Dive into the essence of creation,
but let creation itself alone.

All Through the Day

Look deeply into things
and discover God there.

My Day Is Ending

Let the day's concerns go.

Focus upon your breathing,
simply observing it.

How did you find God in your life today?

How might you have found God there?

Night Prayer

Gracious God,
give me the discipline
to seek you in everything
and in everyone I encounter.
Teach me that not one minute
is wasted if I recognize
that it draws me toward you.

Day Seven

My Day Begins

Watching for the Lord

As Jesus told us,
"Be always on guard, expecting the Lord."
Watchful people are always vigilant,
constantly ready to receive the expected one,
always ready to discover him in whatever happens;
nothing is so strange,
but that we should not expect him there.
Such awareness calls for an effort

that taxes our abilities to the utmost.
We want to find God equally present in everything,
as much in one thing as in another.
Sure, one kind of work differs from another,
but if we take the same stance
toward each of our various tasks,
they will be all the same to us.
No one action is less sacred than another.
We will shine forth with the divine light
in the secular world as much as in the sacred.

This does not mean
that we should act in a worldly way,
but that whatever happens to us
we should see it in the light of God.
You have two choices in the spiritual life:

learn to have God in your everyday life
and keep God's presence there,
or give up the world entirely.
Now the latter is not a real option, so we must learn
to keep God in all we do,
whatever the job,
whatever the circumstances.
Let nothing hinder you in this.
So when you are starting out on this path
and have to interact with other people,
first commit yourself strongly to God
and plant God soundly in your heart;
unite all your being with God,
so that nothing else
can distract you from God.

All Through the Day

Let me find God equally present
in everything.

My Day Is Ending

Where did you feel present to God today?

Where did you feel distant from God?

In your imagination now
picture those times of absence
as times of presence.

How is God present even
in seeming absence?

Night Prayer

Thank you for showing
me your presence with me today.
May I come to sense your presence
in everything I do.
May I see all my activities
as filled with you,
and realize that nothing is alien to you.

Day Eight

◆◆◆◆◆

My Day Begins

The Meaning of Good Will

It is impossible to lose God
as long as you have good will.
Of course it is easy for us to think
that we have lost God.
What should you do when this thought arises?
Act as though you are quite confident and secure.
Practice acting this way
even when you are in the utmost distress,

and maintain this stance in each of life's situations.
There is no better counsel that I can give
but to assure you that you will find God
where you lost God.
Remember how you last possessed God
and act the same way now
when you think you have lost God,
and you will find God again.

People say they have good will,
but they do not have God's will;
they want what they want
and would teach our Lord what he should do.
This is not good will.
Seek for the most loving will in God.
God wills that we surrender our wills.

Paul talked back and forth with God,
but only when he surrendered and said,
"Lord, what will you have me do?"
could God do
what needed to be done.
When the angel came to Mary
nothing they said to one another
could render her the Mother of God,
but as soon as she gave up her will,
she mothered the Eternal Word,
giving flesh to God as her natural Son.

You cannot be truly yourself
unless you give up your own will.
Apart from such surrender
there is no real encounter with God.

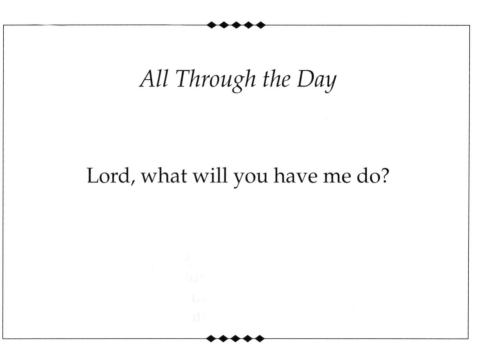

All Through the Day

Lord, what will you have me do?

GOD AWAITS YOU

My Day Is Ending

When today were you most full of yourself?
When were you most full of God?

In remembrance allow both experiences
to unfold.
Which was most satisfying to you?

What would it be like to be most full of God
in that time when you were
most full of yourself?

Night Prayer

Lord, help me to surrender
to you completely.
I know that my happiness
lies in you.
Be patient with me
and guide me.
I am confident you are with me
in every moment
whether I am filled with myself or you.

Day Nine

My Day Begins
Surrender of the Will

You hear of people who want great experiences.
They want such and such to happen,
they want this good thing.
This is nothing but self-will.
Surrender totally to God
and then be content
with whatever God does with God's own.
Thousands have gone to heaven
without really surrendering their own will.
The only true will

is that which has merged with God's will,
so that no will of one's own remains.
The more this is true,
the more you blend into God.
One step taken in surrender to the divine will
is worth more than an ocean journey without it.
When you are merged with God,
if anyone would touch you
they must first touch God.
God becomes like your clothing;
to touch you
a person must first touch your garment.
No matter how serious the difficulty,
if it comes through God,
God is stricken first.

No pain ever befell a human being,
no matter how light or heavy,
which did not affect God
infinitely more than that mortal,
and was not endlessly more adverse for God.
So, if God puts up with it out of some good
he foresees for you,
and if you are willing to undergo
what God undergoes,
and to receive what comes to you from God,
then whatever you receive
becomes divine in itself.
Shame turns into honor, bitterness grows sweet,
darkness transforms into clear light.

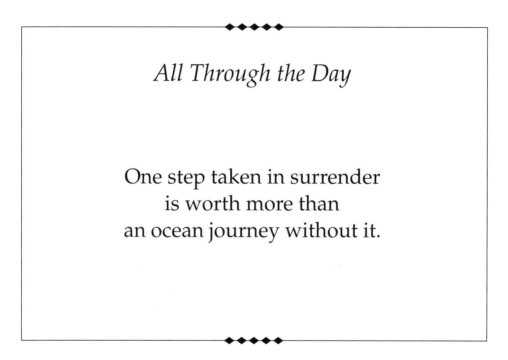

All Through the Day

One step taken in surrender
is worth more than
an ocean journey without it.

My Day Is Ending

Take a few moments to relax
and remember your day.

Can you remember times of surrender?

Times when you might have surrendered?

What stopped you?

Would it have helped to surrender?

Night Prayer

Lord, help my will
blend into yours.
Be my protection,
my clothing.
Make me all your own.

Day Ten

My Day Begins

All Works to the Good

All that is
receives its flavor from God and is divinized.
But all things betray God
when your mind is out of joint.
Everything shares one taste
and God is the same to you
whether this be one of life's bitterest moments
or sweetest pleasures.

The light shines in the darkness
and in the darkness
we become conscious of it.
What good is either light or knowledge
unless it is used?
When people are in the dark, or in suffering,
it is then
that they are to see the light.

In truth, the more we are ourselves,
the less self there is in us.
A person who denies oneself
never wanders from God
whatever he or she does.
If you make mistakes, tell lies, do what is wrong,
if God is your foundation,

God will assume the blame.
So such things should not get in the way of our work.
Such failures and failings are part of this life
and we shall never escape them.
You do not cast out the good grain
just because it is often invaded by rats.
To a friend of God,
suffering and unexpected calamities
can bear fruit,
for everything,
including sin,
works together for the good.

All Through the Day

Everything, including sin,
works together for the good.

My Day Is Ending

After taking some time to relax
and let go of today's problems,
look back on your life
to troublesome times.

How was God there for you then?

Did you see the light in your darkness?

Was it only later you recognized the light?

Night Prayer

Gracious God,
help me to realize
that you are with me
in light and in darkness,
through thick and thin,
in good times and in bad.
I want to celebrate
your presence in all my life.

Day Eleven

◆◆◆◆◆

My Day Begins

Sin as Opportunity

It is not sin if we have sinned and then repent of it.
Just do not consent to sin for any reason whatever.
People steadfast in God know that God,
faithful and loving, has brought them out of a sinful life
into one that is divine.
Such is the motivation of one who seeks God,
and when you completely deny yourself,
such denial multiplies the power of love.

When you are joined to God's will
you will not wish that a sin had never occurred.

Yes, it was against God,
but through the sin you are committed to greater love.
The humility we find in the sin
raises us in the love of God.
God put the sin in your way
only to bring out the best in you.
So when you come to your senses
and abandon it and rise above,
the ever faithful God sees you
as if you had never sinned at all.
Not for an instant does God allow
those former sins to weigh against you.
It matters not the number of sins or their magnitude.

It could be all the sins in the world,
still God would not count them against you,
and God would have as much trust in you
as in any other creature.
When God finds you ready,
no attention is paid to what you were.
God is God of the present:
as God finds you now, so God accepts you,
not for what you have been but for who you are.
God will gladly suffer all the evil, sin, violence you can do
now and for years to come,
awaiting only the chance to convince you of God's love,
to earn your affection and gratitude,
and make your struggle more heartfelt.
And such an opportunity often arises after sin.

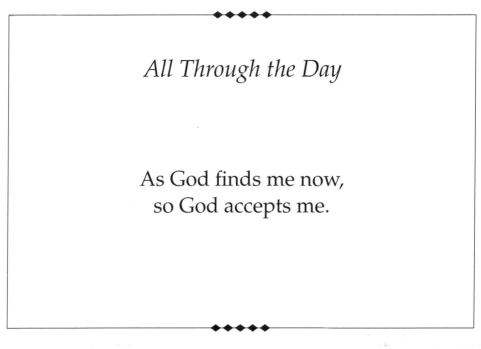

All Through the Day

As God finds me now,
so God accepts me.

GOD AWAITS YOU

My Day Is Ending

Tonight after you have let go of the day
reflect upon your failings or sins.

How do you relate to them?

Do they discourage you?

Can you overlook them?

Can you see them
as ways of drawing nearer to God?

Night Prayer

Lord,
everything in my life
can be a teaching
and a means
of coming closer to you.
Give me the confidence
and the hope
that whatever I encounter
brings me closer
to your will and love.

Day Twelve

◆◆◆◆◆

My Day Begins
From Sin to Repentance

God puts up with sin gladly
and endures much of it.
Frequently, God allows us to sin
because God knows already that by sinning
we will transcend our present state.
For example, who was more in love
or intimate with our Lord than his disciples?
Yet not one of them did not fall into deadly sin;
every one was a mortal sinner.

Throughout the scriptures
we find that the greatest sinners
come to love God most truly.
Even today, you don't hear
about people accomplishing great things
without first making great errors.
God wishes us to learn from this experience
the greatness of God's compassion for us
so that we might be moved toward
greater humility and loyalty.
Each time we repent
love is made anew and increases.
But what is repentance?
One kind which is earthly
pulls us down into ever greater sorrow,

leads us to complain, and delivers us into doubt.
Such repentance is mired in misery
and goes nowhere.
Divine repentance is entirely different.
Not content with ourselves,
we rise up at once to God, and we turn our backs
on all sin with an adamant will.
As we rise toward God we gain certitude
and bask in a spiritual joy
that lifts us above all misery
and joins us to God.
And the weaker we are,
the more we have sinned,
the more we feel
we must bind ourselves to God in pure love.

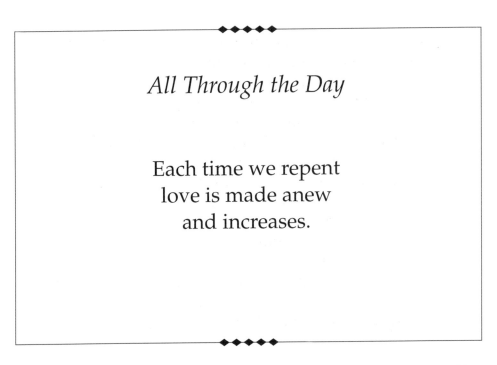

All Through the Day

Each time we repent
love is made anew
and increases.

My Day Is Ending

Once you have relaxed
from your day
take a look at the
two kinds of repentance.

Which is more your style?

In your imagination
picture repenting the second way,
in joy and confidence.

Night Prayer

God of love,
all roads, all events
lead only to you.
Teach me
to see all things
as given by you
to bring all creation
closer to you.

Day Thirteen

◆◆◆◆◆

My Day Begins

Trust and Confidence

The worse you believe your sins to be,
the more ready God is to pardon them.
God wishes to enter your soul
and drive them out;
for no one is a laggard in rooting out
what is loathsome to him.
The more sins you have
the happier God is to forgive them.

And the more displeasing they are to God,
the quicker God forgives.
As soon as your repentance mounts up to God
your sins are swallowed up
in the abyss of God,
quicker than you can blink your eyes.

You demonstrate true and perfect love
when you have great hope and trust in God.
Nothing proves the fullness of love
better than trust.
When you love another with all your heart
you have confidence.
Whatever trust you place in God
is guaranteed,
and you find your trust rewarded a thousand times.

Just as you cannot love God too much,
you are never in danger of putting
too much confidence in God.
You can do nothing better
than to place your complete trust in God.
God has never let anyone down
who trusted fully.
Indeed through you
God will accomplish great things.
When we have this great trust
we become aware
that it arises out of love.
For love bears not only trust
but real knowledge
and absolute certainty.

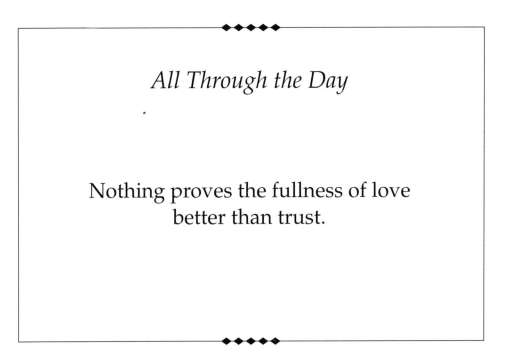

All Through the Day

Nothing proves the fullness of love
better than trust.

God Awaits You

My Day Is Ending

After relaxing, consider the extent
to which you trust God
with your life.

What has helped your trust grow?

What obstructs your trust now?

How does that trust translate
to other people?

Just who do you trust?

Night Prayer

Great God,
you are my hope,
you are my trust,
you are my love.
My life is in your hands.
Show me how
you would have me live
to bring me closer to you.

Day Fourteen

My Day Begins

Confidence of Eternal Life

We can have two kinds of certainty
about eternal life.
The first is the belief that God has told us about it
through some special revelation.
This is rare.
The second kind is much more useful
and is common among people who love completely.
It is grounded on our love for God

and our intimacy with him which so joins us to God
that we trust God completely
and love God without distinction in all creatures.

Love entails a confidence in the good
and once you discover that God is your friend
you know what is good for you
and what makes you happy.
Be certain of this:
no matter how dear you are to God,
God is infinitely dearer to you
and trusts you that much more;
for God himself is the trust
by which we are confident in him.
Now perfect confidence and love
cannot coexist with sins,

rather they hide sin completely.
Love knows nothing of sin.
Love blots it out
and it disappears as though it never was.
Whatever God accomplishes
is accomplished totally,
like a cup running over.
God will always choose great forgiveness
over little forgiveness.
Neither sin nor anything else
can be an obstacle to God's love.
And God rates his lovers as equals
whether their sins are few or many.
To be forgiven much is to love much
as our Lord Jesus pointed out.

Day Fourteen

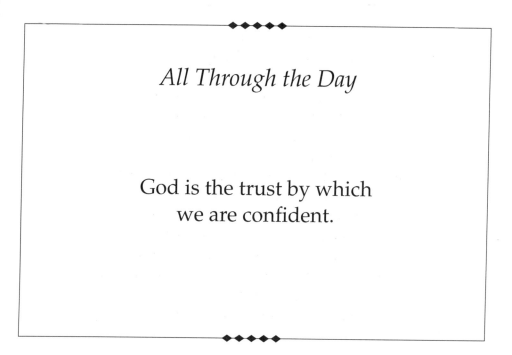

All Through the Day

God is the trust by which
we are confident.

God Awaits You

My Day Is Ending

Review your day today
and in your imagination
double the amount of trust
which you had.

What might such a day have been like?

Night Prayer

Lord, lead me upon
the path of trust in you.
Help me to see
that the trust I have in you
is actually you
extending yourself
in love to me
and all creation.

Day Fifteen

My Day Begins

True Penitence

Many people think that to be sorry
they must do extraordinary things
such as fasting, walking barefoot, and the like.
The best penitence, however, is
to turn away completely
from all that is not God and not divine,
whether it be in yourself
or any other creature.

True repentance is to face God squarely
with constant love,
so that whatever we think
or take pleasure in is pregnant with God.
However you do this is your way,
and the more you do it
the more real your repentance is.
Real conversion is like this
and is best seen in our Lord's passion.
The more you imitate that
the more your sins fall away
along with the pain they cause you.
Make it your life's project to copy Jesus,
what he did
as well as what he refused to do,

his life and passion.
Keep him in mind at all times,
just as he constantly remembered us.
This penitence is simply a consciousness
which is raised
above all creatures to God alone;
whatever exercises or techniques help you do this,
commit yourself to them faithfully.
Whatever hinders this consciousness,
stop it at once,
and do not worry
whether your penitence is being neglected.
God isn't interested in what you do
but only in the quality of love and devotion
which supports your actions.

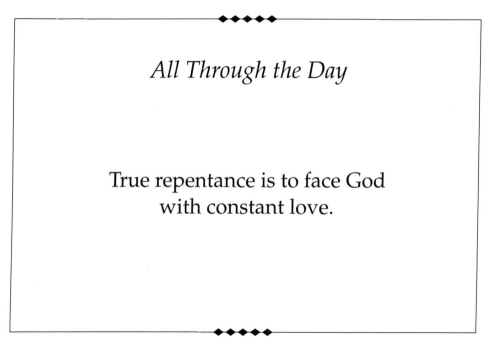

All Through the Day

True repentance is to face God
with constant love.

My Day Is Ending

Take some time to reflect upon
those things in your life
that draw you closer to God.

What things draw you away from God?

How might you increase those things
that bring you closer to God?

Night Prayer

Lord, help me to let go of
all that makes me feel far from you.
Draw me ever closer to you.
May love and devotion
be in all my actions,
so that others may come to know
of your glory.

Day Sixteen

◆◆◆◆◆

My Day Begins

Finding Your Path

People sometimes become anxious and discouraged
when they look at the lives of Jesus and the saints,
because they believe they are not as holy;
and in truth they do not even want to be.
When people think they are not in this company,
they assume that they are cut off from God
and do not have confidence they can be disciples.
Never think this way!

Nobody at any time is cut off from God,
either because of imperfections or weakness
or anything else.
And if because of circumstance
you find yourself ostracized from others,
then especially believe that God is near you,
for thinking God far away brings great hurt to you.
Whether you go away or return, God never leaves you.
God is always present and if God cannot enter your life,
he is no farther away than the door.

Now let us consider
the difficult and hard life of discipleship.
First of all, notice just what God calls you to do;
all people are not called to God by the same path.
You may find that your shortest route

is not by actions
or great discipline.
These after all are of no importance,
unless you are particularly
summoned by God to them—
which means you are strong enough
to endure such a way
without harm to your spiritual life.
But if such is not your path,
be at peace about it and move on.
You may admire the lives of such spiritual warriors,
but it does you no good to envy them
or wish you could be them:
it is not your way.

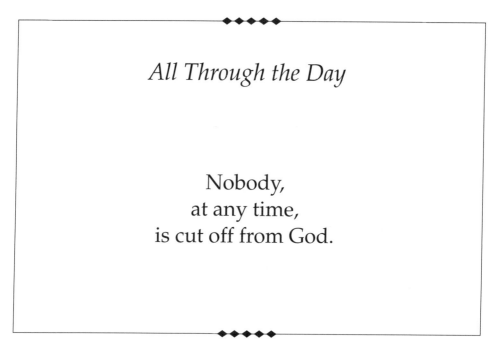

All Through the Day

Nobody,
at any time,
is cut off from God.

GOD AWAITS YOU

My Day Is Ending

Take some time to reflect upon
how you might have avoided
getting close to God
because you couldn't measure
up to someone you considered holy.

Now reflect upon the path
God is calling you to follow.

Can you walk this path?
What attracts you to it?
What about it scares you?

Night Prayer

Great God,
I thank you
for the assurance that
you will never be far from me.
Help me to find the path
you have set for me,
and give me the courage
to walk it.

Day Seventeen

My Day Begins

Need for Intelligence

Perhaps you believe
that the path of Jesus is the best
and we must always follow him.
This is true,
but we are meant to follow Jesus intelligently,
not simply by duplicating his every action.
For instance,
Jesus fasted for forty days and nights.

No one is asked to copy him literally in this.
As in many other things he accomplished,
he intended that we should follow him
in spirit, but not to the letter.
You must always use your mother wit
on your spiritual path;
Jesus is much more interested in your love
than in your accomplishments.

You must follow Christ in your own way.
And what is this?
The specific regimen and techniques
need to be determined for each person individually.
Action with intelligence is
always preferred to literal imitation.
So what does this mean?

Jesus fasted forty days.
Follow him by taking some bad habit
and refrain from indulging it.
But pay attention:
it is preferable to drop that habit without regret
than to give up food completely.
And realize that
it is often harder to keep back one angry word
that to refrain from speaking altogether,
harder to be alone in a crowd
than in a desert,
harder to complete one little task
than an important one.
Through your weakness you may follow Jesus
and need not believe he is far away from you.

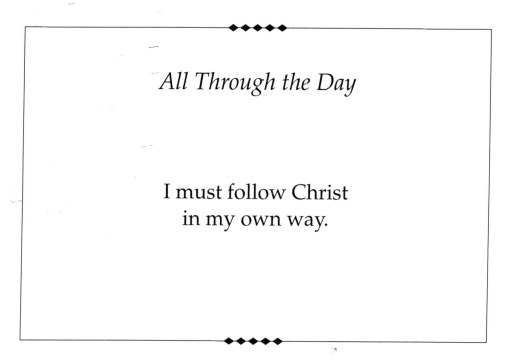

All Through the Day

I must follow Christ
in my own way.

My Day Is Ending

Take a few minutes to relax
and look back over your day.

Where today did you see hints
of how you should follow Jesus?

What bad habit are you truly willing
to be freed from?
How might you go about breaking this habit?
How will you check your progress?

Night Prayer

God, help me to see
your particular path for me.
Open my eyes to what is
happening in my life.
Give me the insight to see
what holds me back,
and the grace to let it go.

Day Eighteen

My Day Begins

Give Yourself over to God

Do not concern yourself
about clothing or food,
or they may come to assume
too much importance for you.
Instead, train your mind and heart
to rise above these things,
so that nothing motivates you
except God alone.

Why?
Only a weak spirit is moved by outward appearances;
let your interior being guide your exterior,
only so will you find contentment.
If you are well off, be at peace with it,
but be willing to accept the opposite as well.
Be in equanimity about food, friends, family, health,
or whatever else is in God's power to give or take away.
Surrender yourself to God
and let God give you what God wills.
Accept whatever is given gladly and gratefully.
Take such gifts from God
whether you would choose them yourself or not.
Know that in walking this path
you are following God's will for you.

GOD AWAITS YOU

Learn from God gladly in everything that happens.
To follow only God is to walk the right path.
With such a state of mind,
you can savor fame and comfort—
equally accepting infamy and misery
should they come your way.
Eat with a pure conscience and joy,
if you are as ready and willing to fast as well.
This is probably why
God visits upon those most loved
so many great wounds and sufferings
which God would never otherwise allow,
being so honorable:
for the blessings that arise
out of suffering are many and great.

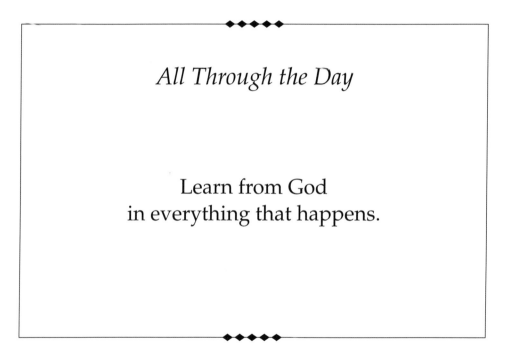

All Through the Day

Learn from God
in everything that happens.

My Day Is Ending

Tonight again consider the path
God has chosen for you.

What are the issues
you need to work on right now?
How do you imagine
working upon those issues?
Try to be concrete and specific.

What part does the virtue of equanimity
play in your life?
Are you able to be satisfied with what is,
with who you are,
with what you have?

Night Prayer

Lord, teach me to be satisfied
with myself and my state in life.
Lift me up from every concern
except your will for me.
Show me my faults
and guide me in overcoming them.

Day Nineteen

My Day Begins

Conforming to Christ

While God does not wish
to withhold any good thing from you,
sometimes God does indeed
hold back on such good things,
and you are left with
only God's good will for you.
Be content with what happens
as long as God is pleased.

And in your inner life,
be so joined to God's will
that you are not concerned
with methods and actions.
Be especially wary
of any peculiarity in clothes, food, or speech
which calls attention to yourself.
For example, do not use high-flown language
or eccentric mannerisms
which are truly of no help whatever.

To be a follower of Jesus
means you do not, in any way,
seek to call attention to yourself.
After all, you are called
to show Christ to the world,

not your own peculiar attributes.
However, there will be times
when you stand out from the crowd.
For you must
mold yourself to Christ in all things,
so that others may see the divine form in you,
which is God's reflection in the world today.
Whatever you engage in,
conform yourself into
as perfect a likeness of Jesus as possible.
You are to sow, Christ is to reap.
Work with attention and total conviction,
and in this way train your mind and heart
so that you present Christ to the world
at all times.

All Through the Day

Today, I am God's reflection in the world.

My Day Is Ending

Take a moment to relax
by taking some slow, deep breaths.

Now consider your day.
How did you show forth Christ to the world?

Recall one situation
where you did not show forth Christ.
In your imagination how might you change it
so that you could show forth Christ?
What prevented you from doing so?
What would be the advantage of doing so?

Night Prayer

Gracious God,
I want to be your image to others
so that all might know of your glory,
your love, and the peace you give.
Show me Jesus more clearly
and lead me to conform myself
to the image of Christ.

Day Twenty

◆◆◆◆◆

My Day Begins

God Our Foundation

Although ever faithful,
God sometimes allows his friends
to become sick,
and allows everything upon which they rely
to fall out from under them.
God's lovers take great delight
in doing things such as
keeping vigil, fasting, and the like

because they find
their joy, sustenance, and hope in such activities.
So their practices become a support for them.
But God wants to remove all such supports
so that God alone becomes their only hope.
God does this
simply out of mercy and pure goodness.
For God wills
nothing more than God's own goodness.
Nor will any action on our part
influence God in the least.

God's friends should give up any such ideas;
every prop is removed
so that God alone may sustain us.
God wills to provide abundantly,

but only out of the Creator's own free goodness,
so that God alone becomes our anchor,
and we who experience ourselves as nothing at all
may also experience
the wondrous generosity of the Lord.
The more helpless and poverty stricken we are
when we turn to God for aid,
the deeper we enter into God
and the more sensitive we become
to God's most precious gifts.

Our foundation must be God alone;
God, and only God,
our help.

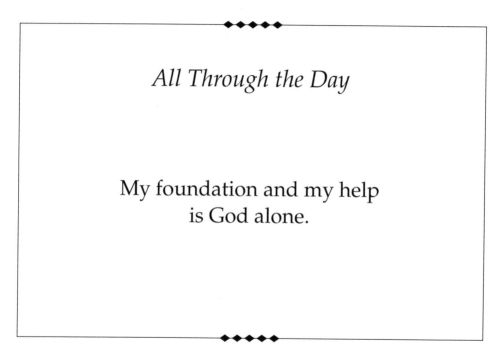

All Through the Day

My foundation and my help
is God alone.

My Day Is Ending

Remember a time or an event
in your life
when you felt the bottom fall out.
In your memory allow it to blossom now.
How did you feel at the time?
Looking back from your present perspective
can you sense God's presence in this event?
Can you see how this terrible experience
could bring you closer to God
and make you more dependent upon God?

Night Prayer

Lord, you are my anchor and my hope.
Draw me closer to you
and allow me to cling only to you.
In your gentleness
lead me to let go of whatever
other supports I have
and to cling only to you—my hope.

Day Twenty-One

My Day Begins

God's Will and Our Will

We need to learn
not to look to our own advantage in anything;
rather, let us be concerned only for the advantage of God.
God has never given a gift to us
so that we might hold onto it and find satisfaction in it.
God bestows all gifts,
whether in heaven or on earth,
only so that the one gift might be better received.

And what gift is this?
That gift is God's self.
Whatever other gifts are granted us,
God is only trying to prepare us
for the favor that is God's self.
Whatever God has accomplished
either above or below
was done solely for the sake of this single gift:
the fulfillment of our happiness.

So you need to learn how to see
through every grace and event to God who is behind all,
and you must never be satisfied with the thing itself.
There is no resting place in this world.
That has never existed for anybody,
no matter how holy they became.

Be prepared always
for the gifts of God, new gifts continually.
Let God's gifts wean you away from selfishness
and help you let go of concern
over what is yours by right.
Desire nothing for yourself—nothing—
neither pleasure, spirituality, nor the kingdom of God,
nor that your will be satisfied.
God never gives God's self to someone
whose will differs from God's own.
The more you separate yourself from your own will,
the more God pours God's self into you.
It is not sufficient to surrender once,
you must practice surrendering all the time.
Only then will you find freedom.

All Through the Day

I see through everything
God who is behind all.

My Day Is Ending

Take a few minutes to relax
and look back over your day.

From this relaxed place
remember the times today
when you saw through things
to God and God's will for you.

Recall also those times
when you became enmeshed
in the moment, in the event, in the thing,
and failed to see what was happening
as God's will for you.

Night Prayer

God, help me
to let go of all my own plans
and desires.
Teach me to want only you
and your will for me.

Day Twenty-Two

◆◆◆◆◆

My Day Begins

The Practice of Surrender

Don't be content
with merely thinking about the virtues
such as poverty, obedience, or kindness;
no, you should show forth their fruits in your actions.
Look inward often
with the desire that others should also scrutinize you
and put you to the test.
Nor is it enough to act virtuously

by being poor, or humble, or putting yourself aside.
Such actions should become habitual.
Keep at them
until you have achieved the essence of virtue
so that by nature you act virtuously.
When you live with virtue with no forethought,
and accomplish great things
without thinking it anything of importance,
but simply and solely
because you love goodness,
then and only then, are you wholly virtuous.
Practice forgetting yourself
until you see nothing as your possession.
Give yourself heart and soul
to the total undoing of your will.

When you are in low spirits and depressed,
consider whether you are as true to God
as when you sense God's nearness.
Do you act the same
when you feel God is nearby and comforting
as when you feel abandoned and disconsolate?
The faithful friend whose will is constant
will find no time too short.
When you want to do as much as possible now,
and not only in the present,
but however long you live,
your will counts as much as all the things
you might achieve in a century.
In God's eyes,
you have accomplished everything.

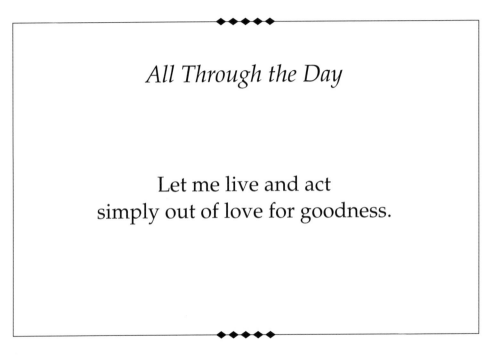

All Through the Day

Let me live and act
simply out of love for goodness.

GOD AWAITS YOU

My Day Is Ending

Take a few minutes to relax
and look back over your day.
Reflect upon those moments
when you were conscious of your
intention to act out of goodness.

When did you forget to act in this way?
Can you sense what got in your way?
What made you forget your
initial intention?
Bring no blame to this exercise;
you are simply curious
about your behavior.

Night Prayer

Great God,
help me to see
all that stands between myself
and your will for me.
Wean me away from whatever
comes between us
and draw me solely to you alone.

Day Twenty-Three

❖❖❖❖❖

My Day Begins

Stick to One Path

Whenever you are about to embark
upon something new—
a new job, a new life—bring it to God.
Ask with all your strength and love
that God will bring everything to a fitting end,
in whatever manner seems apt and best to God.
Make sure you are not considering
your own advantage,

but simply what is God's will, and only that.
Then whatever God makes happen,
take that as your answer.
This is most appropriate for you as God sees it.
Be totally contented.
Perhaps later a better solution will occur to you.
If so, think of this
as a better way which God means for you.
Trust in God, and whatever you do,
use everything, no matter what,
to further join your will to God's.

God always sends us what is good and best for us,
but we receive that good
in a great variety of ways.
All good ways of perfection

come together in the one way.
And that one way
is not exclusive to any one method.
You have to decide to do one thing;
you cannot do everything.
You will always be one individual,
but you can absorb everything into yourself.
If you shift back and forth among methods,
choosing whatever pleases you at the moment,
you will become unstable.
Choose one good path for yourself
and cling to it always.
Do not forget that all ways are of God.
Don't begin upon one path today
and choose another tomorrow.

All Through the Day

All I do today
is in keeping with God's will.

My Day Is Ending

Eckhart speaks of
choosing one path and making it your own.
Spend your time tonight
discerning what your
path and method is.

How does this method nourish you?
How does it challenge you?
How does it further
your alignment to God's will?

Night Prayer

God of my hope,
all paths lead to you.
Help me to choose my way
and give me the patience
to persevere in that way
through all the obstacles,
until I belong to you alone.

Day Twenty-Four

◆◆◆◆◆

My Day Begins

The Path Untaken

When you settle upon a spiritual practice or path
do not fret that by doing so
you are missing out on something.
As long as you are with God you will not miss anything;
for since God by nature is unlikely to miss something,
so we are unlikely to overlook something
when we are joined to God.
Therefore set out upon your own path

as it is given you by God, and trust
that it will include all good paths in itself.
However, if you are unable
to reconcile one good way with another,
take it as a sure sign
that one of the two is not of God.

One good does not conflict with another;
when a greater good collides with a lesser one,
one of them is not of God.
Good builds up; it does not destroy.
The truth is
that God always provides the best for everyone,
and never accepts a person lying down
when he might be upright,
for out of the Godhead

wisdom discerns what is best for each.
You might ask:
if God knows what is best, why would God
not take a person to God's self in infancy
if God knew that this person
would later fall away in sin?
But God does not destroy anything which is good.
Rather God fulfills and perfects nature,
and would never bring it down. _____
Grace does not replace nature
but brings it to wholeness.
We have free will to choose between good and evil.
God tells us the consequences of
good and evil, life and death.
Our free choice is preserved for us.

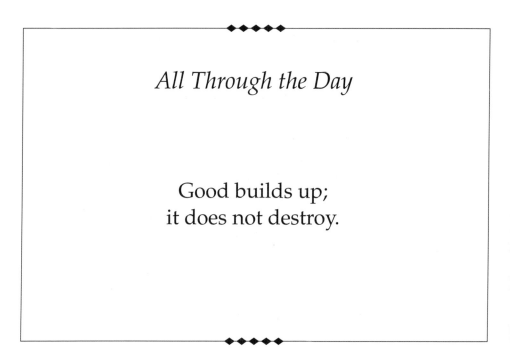

All Through the Day

Good builds up;
it does not destroy.

GOD AWAITS YOU

My Day Is Ending

Continue your reflection
upon the path which
God wishes you to walk.
Is there a conflict between
the different paths you are discerning,
or is it a matter of one good or another?

If there is a conflict
try to discern which path
truly leads toward God.

Night Prayer

Lord,
show me the way
you desire for me
and let me be satisfied in that.
When I am tempted to stray
assure me that this is my way,
and that only faithfulness
to this path will
truly lead me home.

Day Twenty-Five

◆◆◆◆◆

My Day Begins

The Inner and Outer Worlds

If you withdraw into yourself,
using all your abilities,
you eventually arrive
in a state in which you have no ideas,
no restrictions, and in which you exist without action,
inwardly or outwardly.
When this happens, ask yourself
whether you want to return to the same old life.

If you have no such desire
then rouse yourself out of this state
and get back to work of some kind,
mental or physical.
Never give in to such indulgence
however blissful it seems.
Such states are unnatural;
you are not acting,
but merely being acted upon.

This is not spiritual work;
spiritual work involves
learning to cooperate with God.
Of course this does not mean
abandoning the inner life;
no, rather you must learn

to work at spiritual growth,
so that the unity built up there
bursts out into action in the world
and that such outward action draws you back
into the inner unity.
By following such a program you learn to be free,
not addicted to or fleeing from anything.
Place your attention upon your inner life
and from there proceed outwards.
If, however, your life in the world
conflicts with your interior work,
devote yourself to the interior.
But ideally the two should proceed together,
for then you are working together with God.

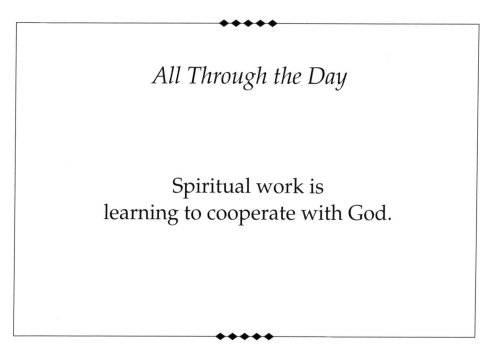

All Through the Day

Spiritual work is
learning to cooperate with God.

My Day Is Ending

This evening, after relaxing, consider the
inner and outer dimensions
of your life and work.
Do you neglect one
at the expense of the other?

Do you notice the movement back and forth
which Eckhart suggests is the true
rhythm of spirituality?

How might you foster
such a going out and coming in
in your spiritual life?

Night Prayer

Loving God,
help me to sense your presence
whether my attention is directed
within myself
or outward to the world.
Teach me the rhythm
of going out and coming home.
Do not let me fall into
one-sided living.
But in all things bring me closer to you.

Day Twenty-Six

◆◆◆◆◆

My Day Begins
Being and Nothingness

Exactly how does a person
"work together with God?"
You achieve this by dropping your sense of self
and your own efforts.
The single action of the spiritual path
is to reduce self to nothingness.
However this annihilation of self
can never be brought to completion
unless God brings it about.

Otherwise, it always remains imperfect.
Humility finds its end only
when God brings us down to earth
by means of ourselves.
Only then will we find peace and real happiness.

Yet such humiliation of humanity
is at the same time exaltation of God.
"Whoever humbles oneself will be exalted."
Humiliation is not a separate thing from exaltation.
The greatest peaks of exaltation are found exactly
in the deepest pits of humiliation.
The deeper the valleys,
the higher the surrounding mountains.
Depth and height are really the same.
The more humble you come to be

the more exalted you are.
Jesus said,
"The greatest among you
must act as servant to all."
In order to be one thing
you must also be the other.
To be this, you must become that.
To serve is indeed to become great
so that the servant is already a great person.
So the words of the evangelist are fulfilled:
"Whoever humbles oneself will be exalted."
To be fully
is dependent upon ceasing to be.

All Through the Day

To be fully
depends upon ceasing to be.

My Day Is Ending

After you have taken
a few moments to relax
by slow, deep breathing,
reflect upon the tension
between humiliation and exaltation,
being and non-being,
slavery and mastery.

Does it make sense to you?

Do you trust in it even though
it may not make any sense right now?

What experiences help you trust it?

Night Prayer

Dear God,
help me to serve you
in all things.
Lead me into the
paradoxes of the spiritual path
and comfort me
when my faith is weak,
just as you give me hope
when my faith is strong.

Day Twenty-Seven

My Day Begins

Spiritual Poverty

Scripture says, "They have become rich in virtue."
But this is impossible
until we first become poor in things.
To come to possess everything
you must first forsake everything.
This is quite just, fair,
and indeed, when you consider it, a real bargain.
If God is to bestow God's very self

and everything else upon us,
so that all is ours in freedom;
then first God must take away all we now possess.
It is not right that we should keep back
even a speck of dust that could lodge in our eye.
For all God's gifts, whether of nature or grace,
were not created
with the idea that we should consider
them our exclusive property.

God has never given differently
to anyone, even his mother,
and frequently, in order to impress the lesson upon us,
God removes everything from us,
both physical and spiritual.

GOD AWAITS YOU

Whatever we have is merely loaned to us, not given.
We are without proprietary rights to anything:
body or soul, mind or abilities, property or fame,
friends, relatives, houses . . . anything.
Why does God make such an issue of this?
Because God desires to be ours exclusively.
This is God's chief delight and joy,
and the more entirely we live for God alone,
the more joy God experiences.
The more we hoard for ourselves,
the less we have for God;
the less we cling to anything else,
the more we shall possess
God and all creation besides.

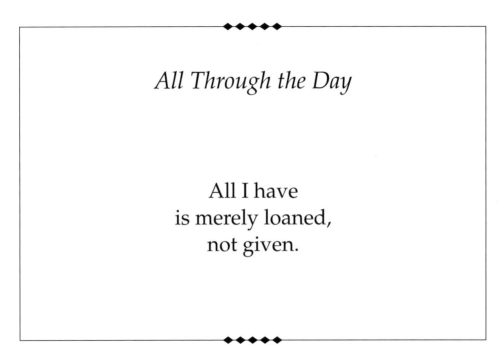

All Through the Day

All I have
is merely loaned,
not given.

My Day Is Ending

After relaxing for a few moments
consider your attitude
toward possessions,
talents, health, and life itself.

Do you believe Eckhart?
What causes you to doubt
his teaching here?
What if anything
draws you to this teaching?

Night Prayer

Wondrous Lord,
you are all I want,
all I have,
all I seek.
I give myself
into your hands,
trusting that
you know what is best
for me
and will bring me to that place
where you are all in all.

Day Twenty-Eight

◆◆◆◆◆

My Day Begins

Poor in Spirit

If you deny yourself, God will be yours
much more than any possession could be.
God shall be yours as much as God's own self,
neither more nor less.
Yours shall God be a thousand times more
than any personal property
you might own and secure in a safe.
Nothing was ever possessed

to the extent that God can be yours,
together with all that is God's, all creation.
And we gain this divine ownership
simply by surrendering our claims upon
whatever is not God in this world.

The more complete and perfect
our spiritual poverty becomes,
the more our claim upon God increases.
But never consider
that this is some kind of reward,
so that you treat it as a profit
to be made or a prize earned.
The exchange occurs
only through the love of virtue as Paul says:
"Whoever owns nothing, possesses everything."

You have no sense of ownership
when you want nothing
and do not intend to acquire anything,
whether of your own or the world's things.
Do not even desire to have God.
What is it like to be truly poor in spirit?
It is to survive
without everything that is not essential.
You will be happier if you get along without things
because you don't need them,
than if you own everything
because you need it all.
A person really enters the kingdom of God
when he or she has enough wisdom
to put off everything for the sake of God.

All Through the Day

Whoever owns nothing,
possesses everything.

My Day Is Ending

Take a few minutes to relax,
then begin to examine
your attitude toward things.

Are you possessive?
About things? People? Health?

Can you find parts of your life
where you are detached
as Eckhart describes it?

Can you imagine what it would be like
to have an attitude of detachment?

Night Prayer

Lord, make me thirsty
for you alone.
Gently draw me away
from all my attachments,
trusting that only in you
can I find
fulfillment and happiness.

Day Twenty-Nine

◆◆◆◆◆

My Day Begins

Contentment

You might wish to argue that your failings
prevent you from following this way.
Well, pray to God
to lift these failings and weaknesses from you,
if that is God's will.
You cannot by yourself escape their grasp.
If they are taken away,
give thanks to God;

but if they remain,
then carry them for God.
Do not consider them as faults,
but see them as your discipline;
and so you will grow
and become patient as well.

Whatever God gives you, simply be satisfied.
Trust that God gives to each of us
what is best and most needed by us.
One coat does not fit everyone,
but must be measured and fitted to the individual;
so it is with our path to holiness.
If you can trust God in this,
you will find that you have enough
in times of scarcity as well as abundance.

Be content with God's will in every circumstance,
so grateful
that his will is being accomplished,
that this becomes more crucial to you
than anything
God might ever give you or use you for.
Living like this, everything becomes a gift
and everything is God to you.
Be so content with all God does,
whether in bestowing or taking away,
that there is no difference
between the way you are now
and the best you could imagine for yourself.

All Through the Day

All is a gift to me,
everything is God to me.

My Day Is Ending

After relaxing, continue the reflection
upon acceptance you began yesterday.
Where in your life
do you find it difficult
to accept your lot?

What would you like to change?

How might the way you are now
be the way God chooses
to draw you onward?

Imagine seeing your present life
as your special path to God.

Night Prayer

Let me be content
with the life you give me, Lord.
Show me the path
in the midst of my present situation.
Give me faith to believe
that you have called me
just as I am,
and just who I am,
sufficient to follow you.

Day Thirty

◆◆◆◆◆

My Day Begins
Is It of God?

Perhaps you are afraid that you do not give
enough of yourself to your spiritual work.
You are lukewarm about your journey.
Well, take this itself as a practice;
be patient with yourself and let it go at that.
God is understanding and easily endures failure,
if only we who are God's friends can be at peace.
And why shouldn't we find peace
with whatever God sends us

or whatever we have to let go of ?
However wrong or lazy we are, if we accept from God
whatever God does or does not do,
as being just because it is of God,
then we can be said to suffer for righteousness' sake,
and we are blessed for it.

So do not complain, or if you insist on complaining,
do so in the knowledge
that you are not yet content with your lot.
Complaining is permitted only if you have too much;
the spiritual person considers losses equal to profits.
But doesn't God act
especially through some people rather than others?
Praise be God for that!
If you are one of those chosen, accept it.

But if you are not, then be glad for it as well.
Consider only God and do not worry
whether God is acting through you
or you are doing it on your own.
If your mind is in God, then God is acting through you.
Do not get into the comparison game.
It is worth nothing in the long run
that someone is better in one thing
and another excels in something else.
Let God act through you and let God do it.
Don't worry whether it is of you or of God;
both nature and grace are of God.
What difference should it make to you
how God wishes to work?
Allow God to act where and when and how God wills.

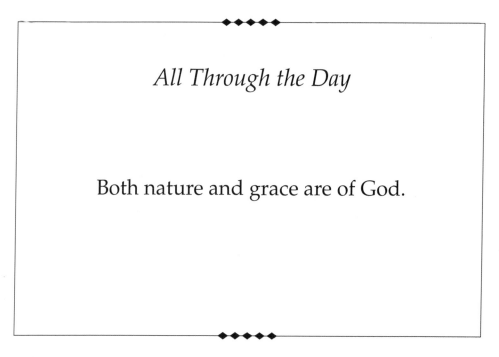

All Through the Day

Both nature and grace are of God.

My Day Is Ending

Tonight look back over these thirty days.
What has Eckhart taught you

about the spiritual life?

How can you put this teaching
into concrete practice?

How is your present life
a sufficient path to God?

How can this present life
become a more conscious spiritual practice?

Night Prayer

Lord, I thank you
for the gift of my life,
and for accepting me as I am
in my journey toward you.
Be my companion
whatever the journey,
and draw me always
nearer to your love.

One Final Word

This book was created to be nothing more than a gateway—a gateway to the spiritual wisdom of a specific teacher, and a gateway opening on your own spiritual path.

You may decide that Meister Eckhart is someone whose experience of God is one that you wish to follow more closely and deeply, in which case you should get a copy of the entire text of his works. Recent years have seen the publication of several, readable translations of his complete works. Read and pray them as you have this gateway to his spiritual world.

You may, on the other hand, decide that his experience has not helped you. There is nothing wrong with this conclusion. There are many other teachers. Somewhere there is the right teacher for your own very special, absolutely unique journey of the spirit. You will find your teacher, you will discover your path. Over and over again during these thirty days Eckhart has reminded us that there is no one path, that each of us has our own journey to take, that every path is of equal value and equal usefulness. "Notice just what God calls you to do. All people are not called to God by the same path."